AF385824

CLYDE SHIPPING
The Twilight Years

CLYDE SHIPPING
The Twilight Years

JAMES A. POTTINGER

First published in 2001 by Tempus Publishing Ltd
Reprinted 2004

Reprinted in 2011 by
The History Press
The Mill, Brimscombe Port
Stroud, Gloucestershire GL5 2QG
www.thehistorypress.co.uk

© James A. Pottinger, 2011

The right of James A. Pottinger to be identified as the Author
of this work has been asserted by him in accordance with the
Copyrights, Designs and Patents Act 1988.

All rights reserved. No part of this book may be reprinted
or reproduced or utilised in any form or by any electronic,
mechanical or other means, now known or hereafter invented,
including photocopying and recording, or in any information
storage or retrieval system, without the permission in writing
from the Publishers.

British Library Cataloguing in Publication Data.
A catalogue record for this book is available from the British Library.

ISBN 978 0 7524 2138 4

Typesetting and origination by Tempus Publishing.
Printed and bound by TJ International Ltd, Padstow, Cornwall

Contents

Acknowledgements

Information included here has been culled from sources and publications too numerous to mention, but it remains to thank all those for taking the trouble to document the history and various movements of ships over the years. Any errors, however, in the following pages are my own.

Last, but not least, to my wife, for patiently suffering many hours on the often choppy waters of the Clyde, also on cold and windswept piers and harbours whilst I waited with camera, always 'Just for the next ship!'

Introduction

The relatively small towns of Greenock and Port Glasgow can justly claim to have been the cradle of steam navigation and steel shipbuilding, with an even earlier history of sailing ship construction. They were hosts to the oldest shipyard in the world; producing Europe's first commercial steamship, the first Cunarder ordered, and the first steam powered submarine. They had a product range as diverse as tea clippers, VLCC's, cargo and passenger ships, tankers, gas carriers, four masted sailing ships, and a full range of warships. Added glory is attached as being the birthplace of James Watt and founders of a number of large shipping companies, however Greenock can also claim the dubious distinction of siring the notorious pirate Captain Kidd!

The area's early significance was due to large seagoing ships not being able to go up the River Clyde to Glasgow until the late nineteenth century, when extensive dredging and deepening of the river made this finally possible. Glasgow shipowners and merchants, denied access to the berths at Glasgow and being rebuffed by the Dumbarton Magistrates, founded a harbour near the village of Newark around 1668 to be known as Newport, later to be known as Port Glasgow, literally the port of Glasgow.

It was thus at Greenock and Port Glasgow that all the cargo was landed, and hence carted to Glasgow and beyond by horse and cart over rudimentary roads, the river passage by small boat being a long and torturous undertaking at the mercy of sail and oar. Even in recent times there is limited access by road and rail to the many villages around the shores of the lower Firth. The bulk of cargo and passenger trade was still borne by ships, from the puffer to the fast paddle and turbine steamers. Later an extensive network of piers and routes served the holiday trade, all stimulating extensive competition among the numerous fleet operators.

Customhouses were active in Greenock and Port Glasgow from the early eighteenth century. Greenock developed a large overseas trade in hardwoods, timber, tobacco and sugar, and at the end of nineteenth century was ranked fourth in Britain for number and tonnage of vessels calling there. Much of the immigration from Scotland also took place from Greenock.

In time of war, the enclosed waters of the Firth of Clyde on the west coast of Britain, with readily available shipbuilding and repair infrastructure, formed a key role in the defence of the realm.

The open waters of the lower Firth were ideal for yachting, and were graced by the largest and most impressive craft.

The present day activity on the river is but a shadow of what it was. The introduction of containerisation and concentration of Far East and Australasian trade from the south of England dealt a fatal blow to the Clyde. Air traffic doomed the large passenger ship, and the coastal trade was also severely impacted by roll-on-roll-off ferry links, the last coastal cargo liner links with Western Highlands ceased in 1976. A bright spot remains however with the growing popularity of cruising, the deep water at all states of tide afforded at the container berth making it a popular stop for cruise liners. Sadly in recent years the changing patterns of trade has been matched by the rundown in shipbuilding, a far cry from when at least ninety shipyards operated in the lower Clyde area over the centuries. The only shipyard now remaining on the lower reaches of the Clyde is Fergusons at Port Glasgow.

A reminder of the volume of shipbuilding on the river will be shown by the number of the shots of new ships on the river, or moored at Greenock prior to going on trials. During the period 1965-1975, covered by the following illustrations, the output from Clyde shipyards totalled 324 vessels of all types, the output more than halved in the succeeding decade, with a total of only 146 ships.

Whilst the busy days of an earlier era have gone never to return it is hoped that the following pages will illustrate the diversity of shipping previously seen around Greenock and the Firth of Clyde in the ten years following the mid 1960s.

Vessels are single screw unless otherwise noted, and dates given will generally be that of time of entering service. As changes of names of ships are of more interest given limits of space not all the changes of owners have been fully documented.

One

River Clyde and Tail of the Bank

Greenock; looking west down river. Nearest is Victoria Harbour used as the tug base, then East India Harbour, with two dry docks formerly operated by James Lamont. The large square building in centre is Custom House completed in 1881, behind are the sheds formerly used by shipbuilders Caird & Co. until 1916, then by Harland & Wolff until closure in 1928. The original Princes Pier was completed in 1870 and extended in 1921. In the days of railway companies and numerous steamer operators it was a busy rail terminal, but by the 1920s with the extension of the railway this custom had largely passed to Gourock. The pier served as a busy landing stage all through the Second World War and the 1950s, being extended again during the war years, but was finally demolished to form the container berth in 1969, its cranes are prominent. Opposite is Kilcreggan shore, with the mountains behind Loch Long.

Greenock, looking up river. East India Harbour with the long warehouse is on the left, construction was started in 1805. Next is Victoria Harbour completed in 1880, behind are the hammerhead cranes and dark sheds of Scotts' Cartsburn and Cartsdyke shipyard. The ship has just undocked from the James Watt Dock, the Firth of Clyde Dry-dock level luffing cranes are in far background, with a semi-submersible drilling rig *Ocean Alliance* fitting out alongside the outer wall. The river leads past up Port Glasgow at far right, just in the picture, and then on up to Glasgow. The large hammerhead crane in James Watt Dock can be seen just to the left of the distinctive spire prominent in the foreground of the Wellpark Church, built in 1854 and used until 1979.

From the hills above Greenock, this view looks across the Tail of the Bank to Helensburgh in April 1987, with Princes Pier container berth prominent in the centre, the new ferry *Norsea* alongside, and jack up oil platform MR MAC to the right. The multi-storey building extreme left is the new James Watt College, as can be noted much of the town centre has been re-developed. The dark line in the middle of the river is the wreck of the *Captayannis*.

The statue of Greenock's favourite son James Watt outside the former Watt Memorial College, who was to cast a long and inspirational shadow on the engineering developments on the lower Clyde. This college was opened in 1908 on the site of his birth in 1736. Whilst not the first to design steam engines his improvements paved the way for the introduction of more efficient steam power on land and sea. He and partner, Matthew Boulton, produced over 500 steam engines. He designed the first dry-dock in Scotland, completed at Port Glasgow in 1762, and a system of waterworks and drainage above Greenock. Many of his tools are in the McLean Museum in Greenock.

Two

The Cargo Vessels

Many of the prominent cargo liner shipowners had their own loading berths at Glasgow, such as Clan, Holt, Donaldson, Shaw Savill and Brocklebank, trading to all parts of the world. A snapshot of a day in September 1962 reveals no less than thirty-five ships of all types in Glasgow docks, in 1972 there were 2,000 ocean going arrivals on the river. Even when bound up river cargo ships invariably lay at the Tail Of The Bank to await the tide before proceeding up river. With the commissioning of the ore terminal in 1958 ships loaded with iron ore passed upriver to the new berth at General Terminus Quay at Glasgow.

Sugar, molasses and tobacco were the main cargoes to Greenock itself, there having been a number of sugar refining and processing factories in Greenock, the first being established as far back as in 1765. The last refinery, however, closed on 29 August 1997.

The main discharge terminal for sugar was at the top end of the James Watt Dock, the last cargo to this berth being from MV *Fidelity* with 7,000 tons from Guyana on 19 June 1992, around thirty ships each year brought in sugar to the dock. The first ship to bring sugar in bulk to this dock was the MV *Carronpark* with 8,570 tons from Fiji on 10 January 1958.

The largest, and last, cargo of bagged sugar was 11,200 tons brought in to the Deep Water Berth by the MV *Bosna* in January 1958.

With the prospect of closing the regular berth in the dock the MV *Kothen* then made a trial discharge of 4,500 tons at the Ocean Terminal at Princes Pier in December 1991.

The first ship to discharge at the new sugar berth there was the MV *Evelyn*, bringing in 8,500 tons from Belize on 20 July 1992. From then on about twenty vessels called each year, the last to discharge at Greenock was the MV *Carola* arriving on 18 June 1997 with 7,700 tons from Belize.

MV *Al Mubarakiah*, 1974, Fairfield Yard of Govan Shipbuilders for Kuwait Shipping Co., was the first of nineteen similar ships built on the Clyde, all engined by Kincaid and Harland & Wolff. First from the yard with a Stulcken mast. Trials picture whilst lying off mouth of Holy Loch.

SS *Anatolian*, 1955, Wm. Gray, Hartlepool, for Ellerman & Papayanni. One of the last cargo ships built with triple expansion engines. Possibly unique bearing her original name on four separate occasions after different periods of charter, under charter as *City of Durham* and Cunard *Ascania*. 1968: Sold and bore names *Agia Sophia*, *Fulka*, *Khalid* and *Gulf Unity*. 1978: Scrapped Gadani Beach.

MV *Atlantic Conveyor*, 1985, Swan Hunter, Wallsend., for Cunard. Replacement for ship of same name lost at Falklands in 1982. This container ship had an additional mid-ship section built and inserted by Lithgows, in the Firth of Clyde Dry-dock, being the last shipbuilding contract by the yard. Note forward breakwater, whaleback bow and raised container stools.

MV *Antilochus* (2), 1949, Harland & Wolff, Belfast. One of the numerous A Mark II class Blue Funnel ships displaying the classic Holt profile. 1975: Transferred to Elder Dempster. 1977: To Gulf (Shipowners) London, renamed *Gulf Orient*. 1978: Scrapped at Gadani Beach. Seen passing under the not yet complete Erskine Bridge, which was opened in 1971.

MV *Beaverrando*, 1969, Atlas-Mak Masch., Bremen, launched as *Rando* for D. Oltmann, chartered by Canadian Pacific between 1969 and 1971 and made twenty-six voyages for them. Seen with some containers on deck but curiously in this shot she has no derricks. One of her lifeboats is alongside, and two of the crew enjoy the view from the crosstrees.

MV *Benledi*, 1965,. C. Connell, Scotstoun, for Ben Line, going on trials. She is fitted with a mixture of cranes and derricks, and a heavy lift jumbo derrick. First of fast 21.5 knots series able reach London-Bangkok in nineteen days, and record passage to Singapore in sixteen and a half days. 1972: Sold to Italy and renamed *Da Noli*. 1987: Broken up as *Tina*.

MV *Benalbanach* (3), 1967, C. Connell, Scotstoun, for Ben Line, undergoing trials. She has a long forecastle with two hatches, Nos 3 and 4 were triple abreast. Another large fast cargo liner which bowed to the march of containerisation. 1972: Sold to Italy and renamed *Da Verrazano*. 1988: Broken up as *Glint*.

MV *Captayannis*, 1963, Nakskov Skips,. V A/S, built as *Norden*, but renamed in 1963. She had cargo of sugar from Lourenço Marques for Greenock when she dragged her anchors at Tail of the Bank in a severe gale in January 1974 and collided with BP tanker *British Light* damaging her port side. She moved to shallow water but later capsized on the sandbank.

MV *Cape Nelson* (3), 1961, Lithgows Ltd, Port Glasgow, for Lyle Shipping Co. Ore-Carrier. En route to Glasgow ore berth with hatches open. The Lyle family connection with Greenock goes back to 1699, but it was a descendent, Abram Lyle, born in 1820 who was to become a shipowner, and also ran a cooperage for the sugar and molasses trade, for which the name Lyle was to become widely known.

SS *Changuinola*, 1957, Alex Stephen & Sons Ltd, Linthouse, one of seven fast reefers for Elders & Fyffes, shown leaving for trials. Last of series to remain in service. 1970: Transferred to Honduran United Fruit and renamed *Omoa*. 1975: Broken up at Dalmuir.

MV *City of Hull*, 1971, Robb Caledon, Dundee, for Ellerman Line. Light ship shows her exposed rudder and propeller. Single mast with full outfit of cranes. After only nine years in service she was sold and renamed *St John*, *Seagull* and later *Sea Lady*.

TSS *City of London*, 1947, Swan Hunter & Wigham Richardson Ltd, Wallsend, for Ellerman. One of a class of four turbine ships, represented the owners at 1963 Spithead Review. 1967: Sold to Greek owners, renamed *Sandra N*. 1968: Scrapped at Kaohsiung.

MV *Clan Alpine*, 1966, Greenock Dockyard. Seen brand new, she was the last Clan ship to be built on the Clyde, and sixty-seventh to be built for them by GD and associated companies, also name of first Clan ship. The sweeping full-length sheer is seen to good effect. 1981: Sold and renamed *African Diamond*. 1984: Broken up as *Pacific Amber*.

MV *Clan Finlay*, 1962, Swan Hunter & Wigham Richardson, Wallsend, for Clan Line. In contrast to *Clan Alpine* she has a flat cranked sheer line. 1968: Sold to Aryan National Shipping Line, Iran, renamed *Arya Far*. 1971: Sold to Tat On Shipping Somali, renamed *Atlantic Ocean*. 1975: To China Ocean Shipping Co., renamed *Lu Chin*.

MV *Clan Ramsay*,1965, Greenock Dockyard for Union Castle Mail Steamship Co. Ltd. Ready for trials and one of four reefers, without sheer these ships suffered in looks compared to other Clan ships. Note vent casing on top of wheelhouse. Last Clan ship to remain in service. 1977: Renamed *Winchester Castle*. 1979: renamed *Winchester Universal*. 1980: Sold to Braganza Bay Shipping Co. Greece, renamed *Lady Madonna*. 1985: Scrapped Gadani Beach.

SS *Clan Sutherland*,1951, Greenock Dockyard for Clan Line and just what a Clan liner should look like. Note new 165 ton SWL jumbo derrick over No.2 hold and tripod post for guys fitted in 1960. 1971: Sold to China, seen in 1979 as *Zhan Dhou* without jumbo derrick and forward samson posts.

SS *Clan Sutherland* in Garvel Dry-dock having heavy lift derrick and mast installed. Thick doubler plates to take the mast stays are being fitted in the side shell plating, a pair already having been fitted further aft. Note fine lines at the bow of this ship, and on *Geesthaven* (below).

MV *Geesthaven*, 1966. First completed at Cartsdyke yard since Scotts' take over of Greenock Dockyard. Lying at Princes Pier prior to trials. Note the unusual and graceful tapered foremast, and pole mast for forward steaming light. 1975: Sold and converted into a livestock carrier owned by Quatar Government.

SS *Colonial*, 1943, Permanente Metals as Liberty *Frank D. Phinney*. 1947: Bought by P. Henderson and renamed *Kansi*. 1949: As T.J. Harrison *Colonial*. 1961: *Planter*. 1962: *Gargi Jayanti*, and finally *Samudra Jyoti*. 1972: Scrapped Bombay. Alongside sugar berth in James Watt Dock with sugar. First ship to use this dock was the four masted barque *Otterburn* owned by Provost Robert. Shankland. The dock complex being completed in 1886.

TSMV *Cymric*, 1953, Harland & Wolff, Belfast, for Shaw Savill. Second of five 'C' class sisters. 1973: To Royal Mail management and renamed *Durango*. 1975: Scrapped at Taiwan.

MV *Colina*, 1960, Hall Russell, Aberdeen, for Donaldson Line's St Lawrence Seaway service. 1966: As considered too small for Atlantic trade an additional hold was added by Barclay Curle, and is seen as such, note new heavy mast amidships. 1967: Sold and renamed *Andrew S. Crosbie*. 1977: Sold again as *Aktian*. 1987: Scrapped at Havana.

MV *Santona*, 1959, Hall Russell, Aberdeen, for Donaldson Line Ltd, a sister to *Colina*. 1966: Additional hold inserted by Barclay Curle, but seen here before lengthening. 1967: Company bought by Ulster Steamship Co. Ltd, with lone *Santona*, Ulster hand badge added to white band on funnel. 1974: To Maldives Shipping Ltd, renamed *Maldive Trader*. 1983: Stranded south east of Port Sudan. 1983: Scrapped at Gadani Beach.

MV *Discoverer* (3), 1964, A/B Lindholmens Varv., Gothenburg, for T&J Harrison. First of five sisters designed for West Indian and Gulf trades, with control cab and unusually wide crosstrees on after mast for Derrick Crane. 1975: To Ocean Tramping Co. of Hong Kong, associated with Mainland China, and renamed *Jinchang*.

MV *Dumbaia*, 1960, Lithgows Ltd for P. Henderson & Co. 1964: Sold to Elder Dempster. Somehow the sloping side screens on superstructure never looked quite right. 1981: To Quest-north Ltd, IOM. 1984: To Chinese breakers, Elder Dempster's last conventional general cargo ship.

MV *Hindustan* (7), 1957, Lubecker Flender-Werke, Lubeck, for Hindustan Shipping Co. One of first UK cargo vessels to have AC current throughout, first British ship built in Lubeck. 1968: To Valerosa Cia. Nav. S.A. renamed *San John*. 1973: To Renata Cia. Nav. Renamed *Agios Nectarios*. 1983 Grounded off Bushire. 1984: Scrapped at Gadani Beach.

TSS *Hororata*, 1941, John Brown, Clydebank, for the New Zealand Shipping Company. On 13 December 1942 she was torpedoed by U-103 north of the Azores but safely made Santa Cruz and Horta, where temporary repairs were carried out. 1962: Collided with the Steel & Bennie tug *Forager* at Glasgow, which sank with loss of two of her crew. 15 January 1966: After collision sank the tug *Islegarth* off Penarth with three lives lost. 1967: As *Nor* at Kaoshiung for scrapping.

MV *Geestcape*, 1966, Greenock Dockyard for Geest Line of Norfolk, registered at Boston. Seen fitting out in calm water under the heavy lift crane in James Watt Dock Greenock, note side loading doors in hull. 1975: Sold and renamed *Nyombe Turtle* she was broken up in 1982.

MV *Kassos*, 1939, Doxfords, Sunderland, for Kassos St. Nav., first of eighty-two ships of the 'improved' Economy Class with design attributed to Captain Rethyminis of Rethyminis & Kulukundis Ltd. A progression of the first Economy class of the 1930s. Surviving the war she became *Marine Trust* and *Lucky* before being scrapped at Kaohsiung after thirty-three years service. One of the Cunard *Ivernia* class liners can be seen behind the stern.

SS *Paestum*, 1944, Bethleham-Fairfield, Baltimore, built as Liberty *Samspeed*. Managed by Lyle Shipping, Glasgow, for the Ministry of War Transport (MOWT). 1947: Sold to managers, renamed *Cape York*. 1952: To Nettunia Soc. Siciliana di Nav., renamed *Paestum*. 1966: At Charleston with leak in No.2 hold, after three days sailed for Norfolk for repair, but foundered off Cape Hatteras. Seen unloading tobacco at Deep Water Berth.

MV *Parma*, 1967, Greenock Dockyard, for F. Laeisz. This and sister reefer *Padua* were the only ships built on Clyde for West Germany. The launching poppets are still attached to bow.

SS *Manchester Merchant* (4), 1951, Blythswood Shipbuilding Co., Scotstoun, for Manchester Liners. By taking a night passage she took seasons' gold headed cane for first arrival at Port Montreal twenty minutes before a new faster Norwegian ship. 1967: To Clio Shipping Co. renamed *Clio*. 1972 Caught fire off west-coast of Angola, abandoned and presumed sunk.

SS *Maturata*, 1955, Wm Hamilton, Port Glasgow, with her sister *Maskeliya* introduced bipod masts and domed topped funnels to the Brocklebank fleet. Uniquely the company proudly flew its blue and white houseflag from the foremast. The bow crest flag was mounted on a door that housed the Suez Canal light. 1969: *Maldive Explorer*. 1970: *Lanka Sinna*. 1970: *Ocean Fruit*. 1972: *Apai Samut*. 1972: Scrapped.

MV *Oakmore*, 1939, Nordeewerke, Emden, as *Levante* for Deutsche Levant Line, Hamburg. Was a German troop transport. Showing an almost Maierform bow, her tall masts and cowl vent samson posts betray her origins. 1945: Taken as prize at Oslo, taken over and renamed *Empire Kent* by MOWT. 1947: To Johnston Warren Lines, renamed *Oakmore*. 1967: Scrapped at Aviles.

SS *Pioneer Cove*, 1946, North Carolina SB Co., Wilmington. She shows the utilitarian upright design of an American C2 Standard cargo ship. Completed as *Golden Light* with space for eight passengers. 1946: United States Lines *Pioneer Cove*. 1970: Scrapped at Kaohsiung. Seen here with some containers on deck.

MV *Sicilia*, 1965, Bartrams & Sons Ltd, Sunderland, the last ship built for joint Anchor-Cunard services. Note Anchor Line flag on badge on bow. 1968: Sold and renamed *Anat*. 1974: renamed *Gold Star*. 1986: Scrapped at Gadani Beach as *Golemi*. Seen docking at Deep Water Berth, Greenock, on a breezy day.

SS *Patroclus* (4), 1950, Vickers-Armstrong. One of Holt's P-class 18-knot fast cargo passenger ships making round trip to Far East in four months. Steam turbines were installed to give the high speed as limits of diesel power on single screw had been reached. 1972: Transferred to Glen Line for period, then back to China Mutual. 1972: Scrapped at Kaohsiung as *Philoctes*.

MV *Priam* (5), 1966, Vickers-Armstrong, Newcastle. One of a class of eight she was made redundant by containerisation after a few years. 1979: To C.Y. Tung, lengthened and renamed *Oriental Champion*. 1985: Was struck by Iraqi missile and subsequently scrapped at Kaohsiung. View shows Stulcken mast on fore deck.

MV *Hermiston*, 1961, J.L. Thompson, Newcastle, as *St Rosario* for South American Saint Line. 1962: To Somerston Shipping Co Ltd, renamed *Hermiston*. Seen with damage from collision with tanker MV *Oceanic Unity* on 14 April 1967. 1970: To Apollo Shipping, S.A. Panama, renamed *Hermione*. 1979: Red Rose Cia Nav. S.A. Panama, renamed *Mario Sofi*. 1980: Trapped at Basrah and damaged by Iranian guns and bombs, declared as lost 1981.

SS *South African Statesman*, 1950. Greenock Dockyard, as *Clan Sinclair*. 1960: Transferred to Springbok Line and renamed *Bosbok*. Pilot ladder and main condenser discharge prominent on port side. 1961: To Safmarine and renamed *South African Statesman* but new colours cannot disguise her Clan origins, funnel cowl on steamships only. 1966: As *S.A Statesman*. 1972: Scrapped Kaohsiung.

TSMV *Suffolk*, 1939, John Brown, Clydebank, this ship was one of a group of first ships built for Federal Steam Navigation Co. for fourteen years, and when built were among the finest and fastest refrigerated carriers afloat. The Second World War had just broken out as she was about to be handed over resulting in her leaving the Clyde without trials. She saw war service in a number of similar roles, latterly as a meat store ship at Liverpool. 1968: Scrapped at Kaohsiung.

SS *Suncampanella*, 1944, J.A. Jones Const. Co,. Brunswick, Ga, Liberty type as *Samaustral*.
1947: Sold to J.&C. Harrison, renamed *Harpathian*. 1956: To Soc. di Nav. Tito Campanella,
Italy, renamed *Suncampanella*. 1963: Marponti Nav S.A., Panama, renamed *Caliopi A*. 1966:
Seawave Shipping Co., Lugano, renamed *Marach*. 1971: Scrapped at Bilbao.

MV *Torr Head*, 1961, Austin & Pickersgill for Ulster Steamship Co. Ltd. Originally ordered
from Harland & Wolff, Belfast, but due to tanker commitments they could not complete on
time and cost. 1972: Sold and renamed *Sheng Li*. 1974: Sold and renamed *Yu Hong*. 1983: With
COSCO/DALIEN, China.

MV *Townsville Star* 1957. Bremer Vulkan Bremen for Salient Shipping Co. (Bermuda), one of series of five vessels. Also sailed under Crusader Line colours, happily Blue Star continued its policy of fitting a large and imposing funnel. 1980: Broken up at Kaohsiung.

MV *Trecarne*, 1959, Wm Hamilton, Port Glasgow, for Hain Steamship Co. 1965: Registered under Hain-Nourse Ltd. With derricks topped and tow lines she is going into James Watt Dock with sugar. 1972: Registered under P&O. 1974: To Golden Arrow Ship. Co. Cyprus, renamed *Golden Arrow*. 1976: To East Arrow Compania Naviera S.A. Greece.1976: Arrived at Hodeidah with engine room flooded, laid up. 1978: Scrapped Gadani Beach.

MV *Tzaneen*, 1964, Greenock Dockyard for British & Commonwealth Shipping Co. 1969: Aquired by Safmarine. 1966: *S.A. Tzaneen.* 1977: *Tzaneen.* 1978: *S.A. Tzaneen.* 1979: To Monsone Reefers Ltd renamed *Papagayo Universal.* 1982 *Asia Freezer.* One of three sisters, she is leaving for trials and is flying her builder's houseflag above the bridge.

TSMV *Waiwera*, 1944, Harland & Wolff, Belfast, for Shaw Savill. One of the 'Empire Food Ships', her namesake of 1934 was a war loss. Originally had temporary accommodation for 100 passengers, reduced to twelve then eliminated. In the 1960s she still had her emergency wartime stump masts and pole signal mast. 1967: To Embajada Comp. De Nav. Of Greece, renamed *Julia.* 1968: Scrapped at Kaohsiung.

MV *Monksgarth*, 1960, Blyth D.D.&S.B. Co. Ltd, Blyth, for Cory Maritime Ltd. Main berth of yard was extended to build larger tankers and four sister ore carriers. Note sheaves on front of superstructures and short pole forward for wires for opening and closing the steel hatch-covers.

MV *Menelaus* (4), 1957, Caledon Sb.& Eng. Co. Ltd, Dundee, for Alfred Holt. One of numerous A-class but Mk 6 type with four hatches before the bridge. First Holt ships to have single-pull hatch covers. 1972: As Elder Dempster *Mano* then *Oti*. 1978: To Greeks and renamed *Elstar*. 1979: Scrapped Busan, Korea.

Wm Doxford, Sunderland, as Hartismere for J. & C. Harrison. 1962: Sold and renamed *Recife*. 1963: Sold and renamed *Carolina*. 1965: Sold and renamed *Tarsus*. 1973: Here at Shipbuilding Industries Ltd yard at Faslane. This site was bought by Metal Industries from the Government in 1946, and repossessed by the MOD in 1981 for incorporation into the submarine base.

MV *Elbe Express*, 1968, Blohm & Voss A.G., Hamburg, for Hapag-Lloyd A.G. The deep water Greenock Container Terminal allowed round the clock operation. This was one of the early medium sized containers ships whose owners used the terminal. However it is now mainly used for smaller feeder container ships and, more recently, cruise liners.

Three

The Passenger Liners

With the Clyde being the nearest major port to North America and Canada it was natural that Glasgow based shipowners would establish transatlantic passenger services. Many of the world's largest passenger liners were built on the Clyde.

Australia and New Zealand were also served, with emigrants forming the greater part of the numbers. Post-war Cunard and Canadian Pacific made calls at the Tail of the Bank, with the Donaldson passenger ships sailing from Glasgow. By the late fifties over 8,000 passengers were being landed at Princes Pier each year. B.I. also used Greenock as a collect and disembark point for their popular educational cruises with their former troop ships.

TSMV *Caledonia* (5), 1948, Fairfield, Govan, for Anchor Line. Her angular lines are emphasised by the severe black & white colour scheme. Built to replace war losses her career was cut short by cessation of Indian service. Was employed as a student hostel in Amsterdam until 1970 when she was scrapped at Hamburg.

TSMV *Devonia*, 1938, Fairfield, Govan, as *Devonshire* for Bibby Line as a troop ship. First ship to use the new Firth of Clyde Dry-dock in 1964. 1962: Bought by B.I. for conversion for educational cruising, and is seen her in this guise with full complement, completing 110 cruises and regularly docking at Princes Pier. 1967: Scrapped at La Spezia.

TSS *Empress of Canada*, 1960, Vickers-Armstrong, Newcastle, for Canadian Pacific, was the last passenger liner for the company. Making regular crossings to Montreal in winter, calling at the Clyde, she also cruised in summer. 1972: After eighty-two cruises and 121 North Atlantic voyages she was sold and renamed *Mardi Gras*, later as *Star of Texas* in 1994 and now *Apollon* from 1996.

One of the Canadian Pacific Empresses steams majestically down the open waters of the Firth of Clyde with the Cloch lighthouse in the background following a regular call at the Tail Of the Bank. This is either *Empress of Britain* or *Empress of England*, as the *Empress of Canada* has a more raking bow and no dark funnel top.

SS *Laurentia*, 1947, Permanente Metals Corp., Richmond, Calif.ornia, as *Medina Victory*,and the first US merchant vessel to have radar fitted. 1947: Bought by Donaldson Atlantic Line, converted by Barclay Curle as general cargo ship with accommodation for twelve passengers on Glasgow-Montreal service, the superstructure was extended around No.4 hatch. 1948-1949: Converted to take fifty-five passengers. 1967: Scrapped at Valencia.

TSS *Nevasa* 1956. Barclay Curle, Elderslie, as a B.I. troopship and completed in B.I. centenary year. When commissioned she was notable for not having traditional B.I funnel colours. 1962: After six years trooping contract cancelled and laid up. 1965: First educational cruise after conversion. 1972: Broken up at Kaohsiung.

TSS *Queen Elizabeth 2*, 1969, John Brown, Clydebank, for Cunard. In Firth of Clyde Dry-dock in November 1968 with some outstanding outfitting work being completed. A design error caused damage to the turbines and considerable delay in acceptance resulted. Now fitted with diesel electric-propulsion.

TSMV *Kungsholm*, 1966, John Brown, Clydebank, for Swedish America Line. A very handsome liner seen on trials, this ship resulted in the greatest loss on any single contract by the builders. 1979: To P&O and renamed *Sea Princess*, after conversion forward funnel removed, this drastic surgery still did not altogether detract from her graceful appearance. 1995: Renamed *Victoria*.

QTSS *Queen Elizabeth* 1940. John Brown, Clydebank, for Cunard. Completed at the outbreak of the Second World War a plan was considered to convert her to an aircraft carrier. She crossed the Atlantic on first voyage straight from builders at estimated 28.5 knots effectively without any previous full power engine trials. Seen here on her return to the Clyde to the Firth of Clyde Drydock at Inchgreen in 1965 for a partial conversion by John Brown with tugs of the Clyde Shipping Co. much in evidence. A notch had to be cut at head of dock to accommodate her. The pilots claimed that the up river passages with deep draughted ore carriers were more fraught than the docking of the giant liner. 1970: Renamed *Seawise University*. 1972: Burned out and sank off Kowloon.

Four

The Tankers

To cope with the boom in large super tankers, Lithgows adopted a method of building ships in two halves and joining them afloat. They could not expand because of the main Greenock-Glasgow road through Port Glasgow. They achieved this new method using technology developed by Netherlands Dock & Shipbuilding Co. in Amsterdam. When carried out on the Clyde it was a first in a tideway. Lithgows, and their successors, built fourteen tankers since 1946, the *British Spirit* in 1982 being the last.

Scotts' and the Greenock Dockyard, with similar restrictions, limited their capacity to about 250 metres in length, and instead concentrated on a mix of product and specialised tankers. Scotts' built seventeen tankers and Greenock Dockyard seven in the same period up to closure in 1983 and 1980 respectively. Medium sized tankers took cargo upriver to the Esso tank storage base at Old Kilpatrick, and large tankers to the Finnart Terminal on Loch Long.

SS *British Admiral*, 1965, Vickers Ltd, at Barrow-in-Furness for BP, was the first 100,000cwt ship built in UK, seen before pre trial docking in Firth of Clyde Dry-dock in summer of 1965. Note what looks like a temporary hammerhead crane on the starboard quarter!

View on deck of *British Admiral* in Firth of Clyde Dry-dock. Note two deck cranes, steam-warping windlass, hinged lid tank hatches and centre gangway.

46

MV *British Hawthorn*, 1964, Hawthorn Leslie, Newcastle, for BP, an all-aft Tree-class tanker, three were built by Lithgows at Port Glasgow. Note that the plating on the deckhouse has swaged troughs instead of welded stiffening inside. I cut it rather fine in my boat to take this photo of the tanker at the mouth of the Gareloch on her way down from Faslane.

MV *British Swift*, 1959, Scotts' S. & Eng. Co. Ltd, Greenock, for BP, one of nine Bird-class tankers built on the Clyde by different builders, the first by Alex Stephen in 1959. She has a elegant arched cross tie in the fore mast, however the exaggerated slope of the side screens looked better on the much larger *British Queen*. Another pre-trials shot.

MV *British Spey*, 1973, Scott Lithgow at Port Glasgow for BP. One of five River-class tankers built within the Scott Lithgow Group, new and on trials. Note cranked line of plating aft. The sister *British Avon*, built at Scotts', was taken up for service in the Falklands war, and took the survivors of HMS *Sheffield* back to Ascension.

MV *Clanity*, 1946, Yarwood, Northwich, completed as Admiralty steam coaling lighter C642. 1956: Bought by Everard and renamed *Clanity*. 1958: A unique major operation by the owners saw her lengthened, widened and converted to a tanker. 1969: Scrapped at Antwerp.

TESS *Esso Glasgow*, 1944, Sun SB&DD, Chester, Pa. Ex-*Wauhatchie*, one of large number of standard war built T-2 turbo-electric tankers built in USA. 1947: Renamed. 1957: New 310ft. long midbody fitted at H.&W., Belfast, for different grades of fuel. 1963: Sank Humber pilot cutter *J.H. Fisher* in fog. 1967: Explosions and fire aboard at Fawley. 1971: Scrapped at Bilbao.

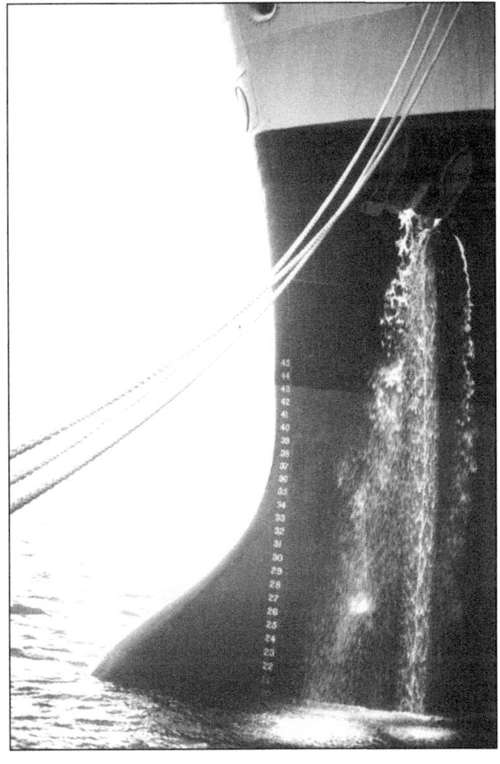

SS *Laristan* (5), 1965, Lithgows Ltd, Port Glasgow, for Common Bros. Repeated engine troubles initially dogged this ship necessitating a three month guarantee dry-docking, two days after return had engine room fire and towed to Hebburn. 1970: To Greece, renamed *Pyrros V*. 1971: Sold again renamed *Spectra J*. 1975: Renamed *Pyrros V*. 1975: Renamed *Yannis Ras Ta-nura*, converted to oil storage and bunker barge. 1990: Renamed *Yannis P.V.* 1992: Scrapped.

MV *Frank* M (2), 1964, Burntisland Shipbuilding Co. Metcalf Motor Coasters coastal tanker which replaced thirty-four year old tanker of same name. Had two diesels coupled to gearbox and single shaft.

SS *Hemimactra*, 1956, Cammell Laird, Birkenhead, for Shell Tankers as *San Fortunata* of Eagle Oil Co. Similar to the thirty strong H-class 18,000 dwt tankers, starting with the *Harpa* in 1953 by various builders in UK and Europe. All geared steam turbine drive except *Helix* and *Helcion*, which had turbo electric propulsion. 1959: To Shell. 1964: Renamed. 1977:Scrapped Kiohsiung.

SS *Nordic Clansman*, 1973, Lithgows, Port Glasgow, for Norness (UK). The vast bulk of the tanker passes the Great Harbour for trials. At time of completion she was the largest tanker built in Britain, was launched in two halves and joined afloat, four tankers being built in this manner. Only ten years later, in 1983, she was broken up as *Al Jazirah*.

RFA MV *Plumleaf* A78, 1961, Blyth Shipbuilding & Dry Docks Co. Ltd. Taken over when building for Cory Bros for twenty years bareboat charter and fitted for abeam refueling. Was first ship to pass through Suez Canal after reopening in 1975. The Falklands crisis delayed disposal.

MV *Marietta Nomikos*, 1953, Scotts' of Greenock for Hellenic Star Greek Maritime Co. Ltd. A popular sized tanker at time of commissioning, and surprisingly I was able to photograph her in the early seventies not far from her birthplace some twenty years before.

MV *Orama*, 1964, Lithgows Ltd for Trident Tankers, with the appropriate funnel logo, chartered for ten years to Texaco Panama. 1974 registered under P&O Steam Navigation Co. 1974: To Brotherhood Comp. Nav. S.A., Greece, and renamed *Ioannis Angelicoussis*. 1979: Explosion and fire at Cabinda, towed out to sea, further explosions, and later sank.

Five

The Coastal Vessels

Extensive coastal trade was carried on the river during this era, regular sailings were provided by most of the major British shipowners, considerable traffic was also generated to the Highland and Western Isles ports and harbours. There was also a significant presence of foreign vessels.

Burns & Laird's coasters regularly loaded steel at Greenock on the river berth outside the East India Harbour for Harland & Wolff at Belfast, there was a rail spur right down to the pier berth. This company also brought cattle from Ireland.

MV *Ballygally Head* (2), 1954, Arnhemsche Scheeps. Mat. N.V., Arnhem, for Ulster Steamship Co. Ltd. 1968: To Antonio Pugliese, Italy, renamed *Ilias*. 1970: Renamed *Ilo*. 1986: Scrapped at Baia.

MV *Adjutant* (3), 1954, S.P. Austin, Sunderland, for General Steam Navigation Co. Last ship to carry clean sea water from Bay of Biscay to London Aquarium. 1966: Sold to Yugoslavia, renamed *Galiola*. 1983: Broken up at Split.

MV *Brookmount*, 1949, Wm Denny, Dumbarton, for Burns & Laird as *Lairds Ben*. 1959: To Belfast, Mersey & Manchester Steamship Co. and renamed *Brookmount*. 1970: To Compania Naviera Vivi S.A. Pa., renamed *Ikaria*. 1971: To Rosade Lines Beirut renamed *Pierre Rodolphe*. 1973: To Khodor Adel El-Hos Beirut renamed *Ziad*. 1979: Renamed *Sweet Waves*. 1983: Sank after shelling at Tripoli.

MV *Frederick T. Everard*, 1954, Goole Shipbuilding & Engineering, for Everard, traded extensively to Baltic with coal and home with timber and pulp. She has a mast & derrick at after end of boat deck for stores and engine parts. 1972: Sold and renamed *Emilia G*. 1975: *Alexis G*. 1981: *Athens Luck*. 1982: *Anna Kassiani*. 1982: Arrived Moita, Portugal, for scrapping.

1963: *Glencullen* under Irish flag. 1968: *Lady Sabina*. 1973: *Tremont*. 1975: *Huziefa*. 1976: *Mumtaz*. 1998: Deleted from Lloyds.

MV *Lairdsglen* (2) 1954. Ardrossan Dockyard, last ship built for Burns Laird. Designed for Glasgow-Dublin cargo cattle trade with extensive outfit of derricks, later trading as far as Mediterranean and USA. 1974: To Frans Buitelaar renamed *Devon Express*. 1983: Scrapped in Spain.

TSMV *Lairds Loch*, 1944, Ardrossan Dockyard, Ardrossan, for Burns & Laird. Completed as cargo carrier only and passenger accommodation added in 1944. In summer passengers were carried on deck under canvas cover as can be seen on after well deck. 1969: To Israel owners and renamed *Hey Daroma*. 1970: Damaged by Arab frogmen, ashore in Gulf of Aqaba and wrecked.

MV *Lairdsrock*, 1935, Hawthorn Leslie, Newcastle, for Tyne-Tees St. Shipping Co. as *Glen*. 1946: Renamed *Belgian Coast*. 1947: Renamed *Lairdsrock* by Burns Laird. 1957: Re-engined. 1966: To Greece and renamed *Giorgis*, then *Lefteris D.* and *Tenaron S.* 1980: Grounded off Karpathos Island and sank. Passing Greenock Dockyard shipyard, the cranes on the right, J.G. Kincaid's on left.

MV *Limelight*, 1916, Rennie Forrest, Wivenhoe, as *Cristo* for Wilfrid Christopherson with numerous subsequent owners. 1958: Re-engined. 1963: To Ross & Marshall, renamed *Limelight*, note diminutive funnel with owners colours. 1966: Wrecked at Port Ellen, Islay.

TSMV *Lochiel* (4) 1930 Denny, Dumbarton for David MacBrayne's Islay mail service from West Loch Tarbet. 1960: Hit rock and sank at mouth of the loch and saved by salvage vessel *Plantaganet*. 1970: On Fleetwood-IOM service as *Norwest Laird* but not suitable 1974: Pub and restaurant at Bristol as *Old Lochiel*. 1996: Broken up at Bristol.

TSMV *Loch Ard*, 1955, Ferguson Bros, Port Glasgow, served on MacBrayne's Glasgow-Outer Isles cargo route, had a distinctive bipod mast. 1970: Glasgow-Dublin service. 1971: To Greece, renamed *Holborn*. Then Spanish owners as *Candiera,* and sank in Mediterranean in 1984, but possibly salvaged.

MV *Lochdunvegan* (2), 1948, A/B Lindholmens Varv., Gothenburg, as *Ornen* with ice strengthened hull. She had distinctive cargo cranes amidships. 1950: Bought by MacBrayne from Dutch owners for Glasgow-Stornoway service. 1951: Refrigeration fitted for carrying fish. 1973: To Greece and renamed *Fanis*. 1976: *Vassilis*.

TSMV *Ulster Sportsman*, 1936, Harland & Wolff, Belfast. Built as *Lairdswood* for Burns & Laird. Somewhat austere appearance, and was built alongside sisters *Lairdscrest* and *Lairdsbank*. 1959: Transferred to Belfast Steamship Co. and renamed *Ulster Sportsman*. 1966: Sold and renamed *Transdropi IV*, then as Bulgarian *Alnilam*. 1970: Broken up in Spain.

MV *Similarity*, 1951, Grangemouth Dockyard, was one of Everards 'yellow perils' and spent long period carrying coal from Goole to Kingsbridge, Devon. 1975: Sold and renamed *Despina T*. 1980: *Crystal Island*.1980: Engine failure and towed to Dakar. 1981: Sank in storm.

MV *Seriality*, 1952, Grangemouth Dockyard, another 'yellow peril' served Everards for her whole career. Note prominent heating boiler funnel aft of bridge and galley funnel on boat deck, also TV aerials. 1971: Broken up at Grays.

MV *Sauvity* (2) 1946. Grangemouth Dockyard, for Everard. A regular visitor to Glasgow, the local Garvel yard of George Brown built a total of twenty-eight vessels for these owners. 1970: Sold for scrapping by Scrappingco S.A. at Willebroek.

SS *Torch*, 1924, Ailsa Shipbuilding Co., Ayr, for Trustees of Clyde Lighthouses. Serviced the navigational buoys and lights on lower Clyde. Steam crane handled the lifts and she was used to shift the navigational buoys opposite Scotts' and Greenock Dockyard when ships were due to be launched, note very tall foremast. Ailsa operated this yard at Ayr until 1929.

SS *Tulipbank*, 1942, Cook Welton & Gemmel, Beverley, built as Isles Class A/S M/S Trawler HMS *Neave* T247. Used as wreck dispersal vessel 1946-1948. In 1950s converted and renamed *Tulipbank* by British Wheeler Process as ship tank cleaning vessel, fitted with stripping pumps and storage tanks. The funnel had red tulip on white diamond, but still looked like an Isles-class trawler. 1979: Scrapped.

Six

The Puffers

The puffer has almost achieved legendary status through the medium of books and TV. The name was coined in view of the characteristic 'puff puff' of the engine exhaust, going directly to air inside the funnel without the benefit of a condenser. They were employed initially as dumb barges towed on the Forth & Clyde Canal, but gradually evolved into a coasting vessel to serve the piers and beaches of the Clyde and Western Highlands, but of a size constrained by locks at the Crinan Canal. The owners had their own distinctive naming pattern, i.e. *light, Spartan, Kaffir* etc.

The fifty-four steam and nine diesel war built VIC coasters were developed from the *Anzac* and *Lascar* built by Scott of Bowling in 1939, these incorporated a much deeper stern and more bluff lines. The larger 80ft VIC's were of a different design, and had flat plates and hard chine construction. The basic design of the steam puffer continued until their demise, apart from the introduction of the diesel.

Puffers *Mellite, Starlight* and *Moonlight* in East India Harbour, showing the progression in size from a canal boat to an 'inside' boats limited by canal dimensions, and the larger coaster type *Moonlight*. The larger boats were built by Wm Yarwood in 1952 and Ferguson Bros in 1935 respectively. It is notable that the smaller *Mellite* has a much heavier derrick and mast.

SS *Cumbrae Lass*, 1923, Scott, Bowling, as the *Pibroch*, and for over thirty-four years carried coal and barley to Lagavulin Distillery on Islay, and transported the water of life out. On replacement by motor vessel in 1957 she was renamed *Texa*, then *Cumbrae Lass*. She steams up river with a light load of rubbish from the US Polaris base ship at the Holy Loch. 1967: broken up.

SS *Glencloy* (2), 1930, Scott, Bowling, for G.&G. Hamilton of Brodick, counter stern and 20ft longer than standard puffer. Telephone maintenance ship at Scapa during the Second World War. During the depression, she was built at cost for £5,000. 1955: Converted to oil burning with new wheelhouse and accommodation. Renamed *Glenholm*, went ashore at Cove, on Kilcreggan shore, and broken up. Her light aerial mast aft seems to have had a nasty accident.

MV *Kaffir*, 1944, J. Hay, Kirkintilloch, one of two VIC type design puffers built there, she was not taken up by the Admiralty but made over to her builders. 1959: Converted to diesel with new wheelhouse and casing. She also joined the select band of puffers starring in the film world when she starred in a feature about the Loch Ness Monster. She was lost in 1974.

SS *Mellite*, 1873, Clyde Shipbuilding Co., built of iron as dumb barge *Salisbury*. 1880: Bought by Ross & Marshall who installed a Plenty compound engine. With tanks built in her lower hold she was used as a water carrier in the FirstWorld War in Loch Ewe and during the Second on the Clyde, in the sixties she carried mails and passengers luggage to Cunard and CPS liners at the Tail of the Bank.

MV *Pibroch*, 1957, Scott, Bowling, for Scottish Malt Distillers, replaced steam puffer of same name. 1989: Sold and coasted around Ireland. 2000: Was seen at Derryinver Pier in October in poor condition in contrast to her former yacht like appearance.

MV *Raylight*, 1963, Scotts', for Ross & Marshall. Seen making as much smoke as her steam ancestors, she was designed for West of Scotland and Northern Ireland trade. Looked like a toy amid the large ships being built at the shipyard. 1973: Stranded in Tarbert Bay and abandoned, but salved and repaired. 1975: Went ashore on rocks off Maidens in Larne Lough in fog, crew saved by Sealink ferry *Uslida*.

SS *Saxon*, 1923, J.J. Hay, Kirkintilloch, launched as *Dane* (2). On 3 December 1925, she sank after a collision off Greenock, and was sold as is to Finlay & Walter Kerr of Millport, who salved her and ran her with coal to Bute for another forty years. She was the first puffer to star as *Vital Spark*, although the *Boer* and *Inca* were used in the film *The Maggie*. The funnel of the *Caledonian Princess* can be seen in the Garvel Dry-dock.

SS *Skylight*, 1936, Ferguson Brothers, Port Glasgow, for Ross & Marshall. The builders also built her sister *Starlight*. With a full cargo and good head of steam heading upriver. Note oil lamp on the foremast. The small boat was usually carried on top of the hatch.

SS *Skylight*. With no possibility of being preserved as a momento after several abortive plans for salvage this example of a traditional type of craft was left sadly to decay in James Lamont's dry-dock. An illustration of the complete lack of any co-ordinated national policy for preservation of our maritime heritage. Who mentioned the dome?

The Ferries

The *Comet* introduced the first commercially successful steamboat service in Europe when she made the voyage from Port Glasgow to Glasgow in about four hours on 6 August 1812.

From this beginning grew the large fleet of Clyde and West Highland steamers, ever faster and more luxuriously appointed, this growth being stimulated by the development of resorts and second houses along the shores of the firth. The regular all year round services were greatly augmented by a fleet of summer excursion vessels. Additional traffic on the river was seen when G.&J. Burns opened up the Belfast trade in 1849 and to Dublin in 1908.

The introduction of the diesel ferries in 1953, followed by the arrival of the car ferry in 1954, led to the gradual withdrawal of the traditional and more picturesque turbine and paddle steamers and excursion services.

PS *Comet* (I), 1812, John Wood, Port Glasgow. How it all began, the small 42ft wooden *Comet* plied initially between Greenock, Helensburgh and Glasgow. Being lengthened in 1813 then in 1816 was moved to the Firth of Forth. Returning to the Clyde in 1819 she was lengthened again, and opened up the West Highland route between Glasgow and Fort William. In 1820 she was caught in a strong tide and wrecked on Craignish Point. This shows a replica built in 1962, which is currently positioned in Port Glasgow beside the main road to Greenock, enclosing fence wire causes the shadow. John Wood was later to build one of the first four ships for Samuel Cunard.

PS *Caledonia* (2), 1934, Fairfield, Govan, for CSPCo., with concealed paddle boxes and single funnel. Operated as railway steamer and on excursions. As HMS *Goatfell* she served as a minesweeper and AA ship during the Second World War. 1970: Sold for breaking up but bought by Bass Charrington for use as pub on Thames as *Old Caledonia*. 1980: Caughrt fire and subsequently broken up at Sittingbourne.

TSMV *Caledonia* (3), 1966, A/S Langesunds MV, Norway, built as *Stena Baltica.*   1970: Inaugurated CSPCo.'s Ardrossan-Brodick roll-on-roll-off service as *Caledonia* (III). First ferry in fleet to have drive through bow and stern doors. Shown after diverted call to Gourock. 1988: Sold, and at Dundee for intended conversion to restaurant ship. Later sold to Italy and operating as *Heidi*.

MV *Coriusk*, 1969, Ailsa Shipbuilding, Troon, for CSP service on Kyleakin-Kyle of Lochalsh crossing. 1971: After being converted to bow loading she inaugurated the Largs-Cumbrae car ferry service. 1986: Sold to Euroyachts of Glasgow.

TSMV *Cowal*, 1954, Ailsa at Troon. The second of the revolutionary Clyde car ferries. She inaugurated the service to Bute via the Weymss Bay-Rothesay route. She was first Clyde ferry to be fitted with radar, and was last ship to call at Fairlie Pier. 1979: To Greece and left under tow, being renamed *Med-Star*, but broke free in the Bay of Biscay. She arrived at Piraeus but never entered service and was later scrapped.

TSS *Duchess of Montrose*, 1930, Denny, Dumbarton, for LMS CSPCo. Designed for cruising. 1965: A sad sight boarded up under tow from Albert Harbour en route to Belgian breakers. This harbour was opened in 1867, and was used for lay up by many Clyde steamers before closure in 1967 to be incorporated in the container berth.

MV *Irish Coast*, 1952, Harland & Wolff, Belfast. She sported Coast Line colours although spent periods in the Burns & Laird Glasgow-Dublin service. Made this unusual call at Greenock Customhouse Quay. 1968: To Greeks renamed *Orpheus*, then *Semiramis II*, *Achilleus*, *Apollon XI*, *Apollon II* and *Regency*. 1989: Drove ashore and wrecked in the Phillipines.

MV *Juno* 1974. James Lamont, Port Glasgow, second of new generation pair of side and stern loading car/passenger ferries for CSPCo. Has a full complement of tour buses aboard. With twin Voith Schneider propulsion she can go ahead, astern and sideways, was built with flying bridge, which was added later to her earlier sisters to give greater visibility aft.

PS *Jeannie Deans* (2) alongside PS *Waverley* (3) laid up at winter berth at outer wall of Albert Harbour. The hull and masts of a submarine salvage pontoon can be seen behind the bow of the *Waverley* and tobacco warehouse in background.

Jeannie Deans' paddle box. She was built in 1931 by Fairfield at Govan and placed on the Arrochar run up Loch Long. She was requisitioned as a minesweeper in 1939 and converted to AA ship HMS *Jeannie Deans* pennant number J108. 1945-1946: New larger elliptical funnels fitted. 1964: Withdrawn from service. 1966: On Thames as *Queen of the South*, but mechanical and financial troubles dogged her and was broken up at Antwerp late in 1966.

TSDEMV *Lochfyne*, 1931, Denny, Dumbarton, for David MacBrayne, first British diesel-electric passenger vessel. Initially based at Oban but after the Second World War she took the Greenock to Tarbert and Ardrishaig mail service, her final sailing being in 1969. She served as a floating accommodation ship at Faslane until 1972, plans for a floating restaurant by Scottish & Newcastle Breweries failed. 1974: Broken up at Dalmuir.

TSS *Queen Mary II*, 1933, Denny, Dumbarton, for Williamson Buchanan Steamer services from Glasgow to Kyles and coast resorts. 1935: Roman numeral II added when Cunard named their *Queen Mary* liner. 1957: Single funnel replaced original two funnels. 1976: Regained her original name. 1977: Sold out of service. 1987: Restored to two funnels, now a floating pub and restaurant at Victoria Embankment.

MV *Keppel*, 1961, Whites, Southampton, for Tilbury-Gravesend service as *Rose*. 1967: Took the Largs-Millport service and was first in the Clyde fleet to have Voith Schnieder propulsion. 1974-1977: Ferried workers to Ardyne Point oil platform yard and was popular charter vessel. 1993: Sold to Inverclyde Marine, and renamed *Clyde Rose*. 1995: Left Clyde for Maltese owners.

TSMV *Maid of Argyll*, 1953, A.&J. Inglis, Pointhouse, the second of the Maids to enter service. She was the only Maid to remain on the Clyde as a passenger ship under the Caledonian MacBrayne colours. 1974: Sold and taken to Greece, renamed *City of Piraeus* in 1974 and in 1996 *City of Corfu*. 1997: Damaged by fire, and did not sail next season.

TSMV *Maid of Skerlmorlie* of 1953, A.&J. Inglis, Pointhouse, for British Railways Clyde fleet. The third of a diesel driven quartet introduced to modernise the Clyde passenger ferry services. Cloch Lighthouse is in the background. Received with scepticism initially but compared to the steamers they proved their worth in all weathers. 1973: To Italy and renamed *Ala* and converted to carry several cars and vehicles in Bay of Naples. 1977: Transferred to Adriatic.

TSMV *Scottish Coast*, 1957, Harland & Wolff, Belfast. Delivered to Coast Lines and registered at Liverpool, but was last passenger ship on the Burns & Laird Glasgow-Belfast run. 1969: To Kavounides Shipping Co of Pireaus and renamed *Galaxias*. 1986: To Vancouver as floating hotel. 1989: To Cyprus based owners, extensively rebuilt and re-entered service as *Princesa Amorosa*.

TSMV *Pioneer* 1974. Robb Caledon, Leith. Has side and stern ramps and was initially for West Highland Islay car ferry services of Caledonian MacBrayne. Over the years has usefully filled a large variety of roles, she called at Douglas Pier in Loch Goil with HRH Princess Royal, and even went as far as Douglas, IOM, during TT Races.

TSMV *Pioneer*, stern view showing stern and side ramps.

DEPV *Talisman*, 1935, A.&J. Inglis, Pointhouse, diesel electric paddler for LNER. After mechanical problems major engine rebuild was completed 1940 and gave trouble free service during the war. 1940: Last Clyde ship to be requisitioned, served as anti-aircraft ship HMS *Aristrocrat*. Chief Engineer Lt. Commander (E.) W. Douglas served on her from 1936 until end of the war. 1946: Returned to service on Clyde. 1967: Broken up at Dalmuir.

TSMV *Royal Scotsman*, 1936, Harland & Wolff, Belfast, for Burns & Laird. Served as infantry and commando landing ship in during the Second World War. Post war ran on Glasgow-Belfast overnight service. 1957: Withdrawn and sold to Scientologist Ron Hubbard, renamed *Royal Scotman*, and then *Apollo*. Later at Brownsville for conversion to floating restaurant, renamed *Arctic Star*. 1984: Broken up at Brownsville.

MV *Sound of Shuna* 1962. Formerly *Olandssund IV* bought from Sweden. 1973: On 3 June after modification inaugurated Western Ferries McInroys Point-Hunters Quay car ferry service. These no-frills drive through vessels, operating from a purpose built terminal three miles south of Gourock pier to the former steamer pier on the Cowal shore, considerably shortened the time to cross the Clyde.

PS *Waverley*, A.&J. Inglis, Pointhouse, for LNER excursion services to Loch Long and Loch Goil. 1973: Withdrawn from service and sold. 1975: Returned to service under LNER colours by Paddle Steamer Preservation Society. 2000: Re-boilered at Yarmouth, last sea going paddler in the world.

PS *Waverley* seen in all her glory in Paddle Steamer Preservation colours and a full load of passengers steaming down the Clyde from Glasgow.

TSMV *Southsea* 1948 Denny, Dumbarton, for British Railways for their Portsmouth-Ryde service. She is shown returning south after standing in for *Waverley* in September 1987. Her sister *Shanklin* was sold to the Paddle Steamer Preservation Society in 1980 and renamed *Prince Ivanhoe* for the Firth of Clyde Steam Packet Co. In 1981 she ran ashore off Port Enyon and was later broken up.

TSMV *Norsea*, 1987, Fairfield yard of Govan Shipbuilders. Leaving Princes Pier for trials. One of the third generation 'super' ferries for North Sea Ferries of Hull. At the time was the largest ferry built in Britain. Introduced a more colourful livery, and arrived at Hull on May Day Bank Holiday, sister *Norsun* built in Japan.

Voith-Schneider propeller unit as fitted to the *Juno* class car ferries. Facing is the tapered input drive shaft, which has right angle gearing to the vertical rotating blades, the angle of each which can be adjusted to suit required direction of travel.

MV *The Second Snark*, 1938, Wm Denny Bros., Dumbarton, for their own use as a shipyard tender and tug. 1960: Cruises on the Forth from Granton. 1963: To Brown Bros. engineers, at Edinburgh, as trials vessel. 1969: To Clyde Marine Motoring on the Clyde for cruises, charters and miscellanous ferry services, now based in Victoria Harbour. 1972: Re-engined.

TSMV *Loch Seaforth*, 1947, Denny of Dumbarton, for David MacBrayne's Stornoway mail service. She was promised back in 1938 but war decreed that she would not be ordered until 1945, then materials shortages again delayed her. 1971: Ran aground on Longay island in Sound of Raasay. 1973: Ran aground in Sound of Gunna with STG Chairman and Caledonian Mac-Brayne General Manager aboard. 1973: Salvaged, but scrapped.

TSS *Duchess of Montrose* (2), 1930, Denny of Dumbarton, for Caledonian Steam Packet. Co., originally with only a stump mizzen mast. Originally taking the Gourock-Ayr and Ailsa Craig summer cruises. During the Second World War she plied below the boom from Wemyss Bay to Rothesay. 1965; Withdrawn and broken up at Ghent.

TSS *King George V*, 1926, Denny of Dumbarton, for Turbine Steamers, Greenock. First Clyde steamer with enclosed promenade deck. 1936: To D. MacBrayne and on Oban-Staffa-Iona cruise route. Made five crossings to Dunkirk in June 1940. On various long cruises after the Second World War. 1975: To Cardiff owners. 1981: For conversion to pub/restaurant but on fire in 1981 and broken up in 1984.

Eight

The Tugs

Tugs operated on the river since the beginning of steam power and a large number were built for home and export all over the world by the smaller shipyards on the river. The Clyde Shipping Company and Steel & Bennie have been the main operators of tugs on the Clyde. These were of varying types suitable for handling of ships in docks and in the more exposed waters of the lower firth, initially paddle driven, then steam and diesel screw and latterly with Voith Schneider propulsion.

The Clyde Shipping Company origins date to 1815, with the first 'Flying' prefix being given to tugs with the *Flying Childers* in 1857. They withdrew from the tug business in 1994 and were bought by Cory Towage next year.

James Steel of Greenock was the lighter manager for the Clyde Shipping Company, and bought a number of tugs from his employer and went into business in 1856 with two sons. David Bennie later joined the business in 1862. R.&J.H. Rea, London bought the company in 1969.

The tugs were based at Victoria Harbour in Greenock, ships over 3,000 tons required a minimum of two tugs for the river passage, and four for vessels over 600 feet.

In the mid-1950s an average of 540 ships inward bound each year were handled by the Steel & Bennie alone, with as many again ship movements in docks, etc., the large volume of shipbuilding on the Clyde naturally generating considerable activity. Duties are currently undertaken by a few Cory Towage tugs, which reflects the drastic downturn in activity.

MV *Flying Duck* of 1956 and SS *Flying Meteor* of 1942. Two Clyde Shipping Company tugs at Princes Pier, now a container berth. The steam tug was formerly the *Empire Dennis* built by Cochranes at Selby. 1947: To Clyde Shipping Co., renamed *Flying Meteor*. 1962: To I.C. Guy and renamed *Royal Rose*. 1963: To Rea Ltd and renamed *Yewgarth*. 1965: Holed by MV *Aldersgate* at Cardiff, beached and scrapped. Ahead is one of the new Atlantic Steam Navigation ferries.

MT *Chieftain*, 1930, Scott & Sons Ltd of Bowling for Steel & Bennie. Note varnished wood panelled wheelhouse and bridge wings. 1957: Converted from steam. 1968: *St Eval*. Converted into private yacht for Savary. The shipbuilders were acquired by Scotts' of Greenock (no relation) in 1965 and the yard finally closed in 1980.

ST *Forager*, 1944, Henry Scarr, Hessle, as *Empire Becky* of the Birch class of Admiralty Empire tugs. Sold to Steel & Bennie in 1947 for £25,000 and renamed *Forager*. Raised after sinking in collision with the *Hororata* and was sold as is to Soc. Rimorchiatori Napoletani and renamed *Mastino*. 1948: To Palermo Salvtore e Cia. 1984: Scrapped at Naples. Three ore carriers are in the background.

ST *Empire Rosa* (2), 1946, Blyth Dry Docks & Eng., late sun catches the tug, which was an improved Stella class tug. 1972: As moored range marker at Luce Bay. 1977: Went ashore, sold for scrapping at Dalmuir and finally Troon.

SS *Empire Ace*, 1942, Cochrane & Sons, Selby, as a Heodic class tug. Renamed *Diligent*. 1961: Renamed *Empire Ace* and on loan to USN on Clyde. Pushing on down river with the Blackwood class HMS *Malcolm* behind. 1968: Went aground on Mull of Kintyre. 1971: Scrapping at Campbelltown.

MV *Spaniel*, 1967. Appledore Shipbuilders for RMAS, one of numerous powerful 'Dog' class tugs fitted for fire fighting and with salvage pumps. Masts can be lowered to avoid overhanging superstructure. Originally based at Devonport and Singapore. 1971: Towed from Singapore to Gibraltar by tug *Advice*. 1972: Based at Faslane on the Clyde.

MV *Farahmand*, 1960, Ferguson Bros,
Port Glasgow, as a fire and salvage
tug. For BP Tanker Company. Shown
brand new, note the wood panelled
wheelhouse and riveted plating
around hawsehole. Sold and renamed
Gulf Span 10 and still in service in
1996 as *Arashi*.

MV *Flying Dipper*, 1958, A.&J. Inglis, Pointhouse, for Clyde Shipping Co. Ltd. 1966: Hit by
propeller of Shaw Savill's *Doric* and sank in Alex. Stephens Basin, salved by *Succour*. 1978: To
Nautilus Continental S.A Panama, renamed *Pamela Joy*. 1978: On fire and sank in Tagus, later
raised and sold for scrapping at Setubal.

SS *Flying Merlin*, 1951, Ferguson Bros, Port Glasgow, for Clyde Shipping Co. Classic modern Clyde steam tug. 1967: To Rimarchiaton Sardi S.p.a. Italy, renamed *Rossente*. 1985: Sold for scrap.

MV *Georges Letzer*, 1945, Cochrane & Sons, Selby, as Stella class steam tug *Empire Martha*, only the after deck is recognisable as such. 1947: Renamed *Foremost 106*. 1949: To Remorquage Letzer S.A. Belgium, renamed *Georges Letzer*. 1964: Rebuilt and re-engined. 1965: Photo taken as she was preparing to tow *Duchess of Montrose* to breakers.

MT *Warrior*, 1935, Scotts of Bowling, for Steel & Bennie. Prototype for early Empire tugs, first was *Empire Pine*, from Bowling, later renamed *Vanguard*. During rescue of the burning tanker *Ferncourt* with the *Chieftain* on 15 March 1941 a landmine exploded under the *Warrior* off Renfrew pier lifting her almost clear of the water. Her engine was wrecked and hull severely damaged, she was later salved and repaired, re-entering service in October. 1958: Converted to diesel. 1968: To Falmouth Towing Co. 1969: Renamed *St Agnes*. 1985: Broken up at Sittingbourne.

Steam and diesel tugs of Steel & Bennie and Clyde Shipping Company fleets in their berth in Victoria Harbour Greenock. The steam tugs *Cruiser* and *Warrior* are on the left, and buoy vessel SS *Torch* beyond, the *Lochfyne* can be seen having a paint up in left background.

MT *Flying Duck*, 1956, A.&J. Inglis, Pointhouse, for Clyde Shipping Company. Note owners characteristic painted ports, compact superstructure and tall galley funnel. 1976: To Dundee Harbour Trustees, renamed *Scotscraig*. 1991: To C.W. Shipping Company, Eire, renamed *Shannon Estuary*.

MT *Typhoon*, 1960, Henry Robb, Leith. Powerful Typhoon class tug designed for ocean towing, rescues, salvage and fire fighting. 4 April 1982: First ship to sail from UK to Falklands, and one of last to return on 24 September.

Nine

Naval and RFA Vessels

Warships of all types have been built and repaired on the Clyde for many years, some yards combining the construction of naval craft along with merchant shipbuilding. Scotts' of Greenock built their first ship for the Admiralty in 1803. They also specialised in submarine construction, completing no less than forty-four of all types. They continued to build for the Admiralty until what was to be the last ship built at the yard, HMS *Challenger* in 1981.

A number of boom defence, salvage and buoy vessels were based at Greenock, initially in the East India Harbour, then in the Great Harbour, to service the many Admiralty moorings in the nearby deepwater lochs, which were also used for submarine diving trials.

SS *Barrhill*, 1943, Fergusons, Port Glasgow, Bar class boom defence and buoy vessel. 1970: Scrapped at Antwerp.

MV A105 *Brodick*, 1971, J.S. Doig, Grimsby. Aberdovey class harbour tenders, steel replacements for the wooden MFV,s, air height limited to twenty-three feet to clear overhanging sponsons.

HNMS *De Ruyter* C801, 1953, Wilton-Fijnoord, Rotterdam. Launched by Germans in 1944, but curiously retained her Dutch name of *De Zeven Provincien*, but took her sister's name in 1950. Both laid down in 1939 but not commissioned until 1953. 1973: Sold to Peru and renamed *Almirante Grau*. Her raked curved stem gives additional 5.5ft overall length compared to sistership.

TSDE *Fulton* AS11, 1941, Mare Island Navy Yard, California. Submarine Tender, underwent FRAM II modernisation to service nuclear submarines, much of previous gun armament removed. Was open to public here after early arrival on the Clyde with transfer of SSBN to Scotland, twin towers of Princes Pier can be seen in the background.

SS *Freshspring*, 1946, Lytham Shipbuilding & Eng., Lytham, Admiralty water-carrier. 1980: Arrived Bristol for preservation.

TSMV *Goosander* A164, 1973, Robb Caledon, Dundee. Later and larger Wild Duck class mooring salvage and boom vessel, able to lift fifty tons over horns and 200 tons over bow. She was used to lay buoys and moorings at Ascension Island from late May 1982. March 1997: Sold to Shoreline Marine Services Ltd, converted to a survey, diving support and cable laying tender.

SSDE *Hunley*, AS31, 1962, Newport News SB&DD Co. Designed specifically to support fleet ballistic missile submarines, (SSBN). Seen in Holy Loch with original hammerhead crane amidships. Tug *Natick* Y60, docking the submarine, is one of eighty-one YTB class large harbour tugs, all with Indian names, and was built in 1961.

MV *Minstrel*, 1939, Philip, Dartmouth, coastal minelayer, pennants M19 and named M1. In another Tempus publication in an aerial view, I note her alongside an HPT ex. class submarine at Faslane. Note large bow sheave and heavy davits. 1942: *Miner I* as tender. 1962: *Minstrel*. 1967: Sold and scrapped.

HMS *Naiad* F39, 1965, Yarrow at Scotstoun. A modified Type 12 Leander class frigate of the first group, fitted with Variable Depth Sonar, seen in stern well of vessel. Forward 4.5 gun turret removed and two quadruple Seacat launchers and Ikara missile system installed at Devonport in 1975. The Seacat and its director can be seen on top of the hanger. She was expended as a target in 1990.

HMS *Puma*, F34, 1957, Scotts', Greenock. A Leopard class Type 41 AA Frigate, fitted with four 4.5 dual-purpose guns. Propelled by eight geared diesels. 1963: Modernised. 1964: Fire gutted engine room. 1976: Sold for scrapping.

SS RFA *Resource*, A480, 1966, Scotts' of Greenock. Photographed after launch which had been delayed by high winds; note bow launching poppet, floating wood remains of launching way packers etc., tug holding against the wind.

SS *Resource* as completed. Fitted with steam turbines she was an armament and ammunition stores carrier, with sister *Regent* were only RFA ships to carry a helicopter permanently. May 1997: Paid off, and under St Vincent & Grenadines flag as *Resourceful*.

MV RFA *Resurgent*, A280, 1951, Scotts' of Greenock for China Navigation Co. as *Changchow* (3) but never served in their fleet. 1952: Bought by Admiralty and converted to stores ship. Sister ship RFA *Retainer* was built by Scotts' as *Chunking* (3). 1981: Scrapped at Gijon.

Nuclear Submarine. Whilst Faslane on the Gareloch had been built as a Military Port during the Second World War development as a specialist base for nuclear submarines at Faslane started in 1962. When completed it was known as Clyde Submarine Base, HMS *Neptune*, with the last of the depot ships, HMS *Maidstone*, leaving in January 1968. HMS *Dreadnought* was the first nuclear submarine to join the 3rd Squadron in 1963. The picture shows one of the large submarines under way on the Clyde.

HMS S07 *Sealion*, 1961, Cammell Laird, Birkenhead, Porpoise class submarine in James Watt Garvel Dry-dock well supported by wooden props, showing torpedo tubes in the stern.

TSMV L3029 *Sir Lancelot*, 1964, Fairfield, Govan, landing ship, multi-purpose troop and heavy vehicle carrier. Was prototype for six further ships. Originally managed by B.I. Fitted with bow and stern doors, internal ramps and helicopter deck. 1989: To Government of Singapore (MOD), converted for passenger and Ro-Ro cargo, renamed *Lowland Lancer*. Seen proceeding for trials.

Stern of *Sir Lancelot* showing hinged ramp and stern anchors.

SS *Spalake*, 1946, C. Hill & Sons Ltd, Bristol, Admiralty water-carrier.

SS *Succour*, 1944, Smiths Dock, Middlesborough. Dispenser class salvage vessel, many of this class were converted to diesel in 1963-1967. Salved tug *Flying Dipper* at Glasgow in 1966. 1973: Scrapped Dalmuir.

MV *Luis Manuel Rojas*, 1975, James Lamont, Port Glasgow, here in East India Harbour. One of five fishery patrol vessels they built for Mexico. The *Esteban B. Calderon* lies ahead; note exhaust trunk openings in casing prior to fitting extensions. A further eleven were built by Ailsa of Troon and five by Scott of Bowling.

MFV 1037, 1944, J.&G. Forbes, Sandhaven, 75ft wooden MFV, transferred to Clyde 1955 and based at Great Harbour. After service many of these were taken up for fishing and suitably converted, others unused went direct. The after deckhouse was removed, most having new wheelhouse and casing fitted which incorporated a galley.

SS A1220 *Olynthus*, 1965, Hawthorn Leslie, Newcastle, one of five Ol-class fast Fleet Tankers. 1967: Renamed to avoid confusion with submarine HMS *Olympus*. 1975-76: Spent eleven weeks on station in Cod Wars. 1980: First RFA to carry out Armilla patrol, and in Adriatic 1993-94. Currently laid up at Portsmouth awaiting disposal with the introduction of the new Wave class tankers.

RFA *Grey Rover*, A269, 1970, Swan Hunter, Newcastle. One of five 'Rover' class Small Fleet Tankers, fitted for RAS abeam and over bow and stern as well as Vetrap with Sea King Helicopter. Original troublesome Ruston diesels had to be replaced by Pielstick engines. Their surprisingly elegant profile is somewhat marred by steep angle of funnel top and black band, which should have been nearer horizontal

MT *Reward*, 1945, Henry Robb, Leith. A Bustler class tug, designed for sea towing, salvage and rescue, the first fleet tugs with diesel engines. 1962: Charter to United Towing as *Englishman*. 1975: Taken over by RN as HMS *Reward* for offshore oilfield patrol. 1976: Sank in Firth of Forth after collision with German ship *Plainsman*. 1976: Raised and scrapped at St Davids Harbour.

HMS *Delight*, D119, 1953, Fairfield, Govan, originally to be HMS *Disdain*. Largest and last conventional destroyers in RN, large size dictated by need to house radar and communication equipment. Originally intended for construction with all welded prefabricated hulls split in 100 units. High-pressure steam employed, with alternate engine and boiler rooms resulting in two funnels.

HMS *Lion*, C34, Scotts' of Greenock, Minotaur class cruiser launched as HMS *Defence*. Last war built cruiser built by Scotts', and after launching was laid up in the Greenock Great Harbour and Gareloch until 1955. 1957: Renamed HMS *Lion*. Swan Hunter then more or less dismantled her and completed her to modified design with the newly developed armament of 6in and 3in guns from the cancelled HMS 'Minotaur' class.

HMS *Sheffield*, C24, 1937, Vickers Armstrong, Newcastle. Town class cruiser,which, along with her sisters, saw extensive service in many theatres of the Second World War. Numerous modifications in light of service in respect of AA armament, etc.; note suppression of X turret. 1967: Scrapped at Faslane.

BB64 *Wisconsin*, 1944, Philadelphia Navy Yard. One of four 16in gun Iowa class battle-ships for USN. Took part in numerous actions in the Pacific during the Second World War and served in Korean conflict between 1951-1953. 1956: Rammed and sank destroyer *Eaton* causing damage to her bow, repaired by using parts from incomplete sister *Kentucky*. 1958: Decommissioned.

USS *Wasp*, CV18, 1947, Bethlehem Steel, Quincy, originally *Oriskany* and one of improved 'Essex' class with smaller island and heavier decks, bulges added to compensate. She took part in the Nato Jubilee celebrations in May 1969 on the Clyde. 1972: Scrapped. Note diesel puffer at stern collecting rubbish, and *Granny Kempock*, ex-61.5ft MFV 137 alongside.

Ten

Miscellaneous

In addition to regular cargo and passenger traffic the river has been home to many diverse types in peace and war. The Admiralty, Fishery Protection Service, Ocean Weather Service and RFA have all at times had bases at Greenock or on the neighbouring sea lochs.

The principal shipbuilders on the lower reaches were Scotts', Greenock Dockyard and Lithgows, smaller yards being George Brown, James Lamont and Ferguson Bros.

The river saw the frequent passage of dredgers and hoppers to discharge spoil, the regular 'all the way' passages of the sewage sludge boats ended in 1988. Some of these had passenger accommodation, and in the summer months approximately 7,000 were carried free of charge. Even William Joyce, or Lord Haw Haw as he was later to be known, made the trip before the war!

Having dumped spoil for generations without any apparent detriment to man or fish, as proved by an independent survey in July 1998, the practice was outlawed by the EC as from end 1998.

TSS *Elderslie*, 1924, Lobnitz & Co., Renfrew. Steam hopper grab dredger, fitted with three steam operated grab cranes, with additional anchor aft for mooring and positioning.

Scott Lithgow yard, Port Glasgow. The 225 ton travelling Krupp Goliath crane is positioned above the semi-submersible drilling rig *Ocean Alliance*. This crane was erected over berth for building large tankers, some of which were built in two halves and joined afloat.

Mixed group of naval and auxiliary craft in Albert Harbour seen from deck of a laid up Clyde steamer. T-class submarine HMS *Tapir*, built 1944 by Vickers Armstrongs, Barrow, is alongside a dumb lifting pontoon craft, with a 75ft. MFV outboard.

TSS *Dalmarnock*, 1925, Wm Simons, Renfrew, cost £48,058 as a sludge vessel for Glasgow Corporation. She was the first Glasgow sludge vessel to be fitted with dedicated passenger accommodation, a tradition dating after the First World War when first used by recuperating 'Tommies'. 1952: Converted to oil burning. 1971: After increasing repair costs was sold and broken up at Cairnryan after forty-five years service.

TSS *Shieldhall*, 1955, Lobnitz, Renfrew, cost £291,000, last sludge steamer on the Clyde. Tables have been set out on deck for excursion passengers, who can be seen on deck just aft of the forecastle. 1977: With entry of motor ships she was sold to Southern Water Authority on the Solent. 1988: Sold to Solent Steam Packet Ltd, still sails as excursion vessel on south coast.

TSMV *Dalmarnock*, 1970, James Lamont, Port Glasgow, first diesel vessel used by Glasgow Corporation to dispose sewage sludge off Garroch Head, but had no passenger accommodation as the *Shieldhall* had sufficient capacity. She had a bow thruster, and the tall masts on deck are vents. 1988: Sold to Northumberland Water, and renamed *Bran Sand* operating between Newcastle and Teesport.

AUXSV *De Wadden*, 1917, Gebr van Diepen, Waterhuizen, for Nederlandsche Stoomvart Maatschappij. Three masted auxiliary schooner. 1920: To R. Hall of Arklow, carried varied cargoes around Irish Sea until 1961. 1960s: To Mr McSweeney, Scotland, took part in 'Onedin Line' TV series. Next owned by K. Kennedy of Dunoon. 1984: Sold to Merseyside Maritime Museum, and being restored with original three masted rig.

SS *Scotia*, 1940, Cochrane & Sons, Selby, as HMS *Fluellan*, a Shakespearian class trawler. 1947: Acquired by Scottish Dept of Agriculture & Fisheries, renamed *Scotia* in 1948. 1972: Transferred to patrol duties and renamed *Scarba*. 1973: Withdrawn, laid up and scrapped at Dalmuir. In James Lamont's dry-dock, note steam winch on aft deckhouse and heavy bollard on the extension.

TSS *Hopper No.8* (2), 1912, Lobnitz & Co., Renfrew, for Trustees of Clyde Navigation. Fitted with older type arched beam with hopper door chains leading to hoisting gear at fore and after ends of beam. 1966: Transferred to Clyde Port Authority.

TSMV *Hopper No.27*, 1962, Simons-Lobnitz, Renfrew. First diesel hoppers on the Clyde, and one of a pair. When proceeding down the Clyde in a fog she inadvertently sailed between tug *Flying Merlin* and towed vessel when it sheered to port opening up a gap.

TSMV *Hopper No.27*, showing hopper door opening gear, hydraulic rams and extension rods, safety stop chains and gangway.

TSMV *Norna*, 1959, Denny, Dumbarton, for Department of Agriculture & Fisheries Scotland. Last Government vessel built at the yard. 1987: *Norma II*. 1987: *Torrington*. 1988: *Isprinsen*, still in service overseas..

TSMV *Rona*, 1938, Denny, for Scottish Fishery Protection Dept. 1939: Requisitioned by RN as examination vessel on Clyde. 1946: Returned to service. 1971: Sold to Hull owners for oil rig service.

SS *Ulva*, 1943, Cook, Welton & Gemmell, as Isles Class HMS *Annet* T341. 1946: Classed as Wreck Dispersal vessel. DV 2 then A 328. 1958: Acquired by Scottish Fishery Protection Dept., renamed *Ulva*. 1972: Broken up at Dalmuir.

TSDEMV *Pacnorse*, 1977, Scotts' of Greenock, for Jebsens, to design by IHC Gusto of Holland. Repeat of the *Ben Ocean Lancer* built in 1976 as the first British built dynamically positioned drill ship. When built these ships were the most technically complicated undertaken by Scotts', and designed to operate in depths up to 3,000ft in 16ft waves and forty-five knot winds with currents of two knots.

TSS *Iris*, 1940, Swan Hunter, Newcastle, for GPO. 1942: Laid first experimental Hais petrol pipe in Clyde as trial for Channel installation after D-day. 1969: Renamed C.S. *Iris*. 1976: Sold for scrapping at Holland.

Iris Bow Sheave.

TSAUXSV *Royalist*, 1971, Groves & Gutteridge, Cowes. Two-masted brig-rigged vessel now owned and operated by the Sea Cadet Association, based at HMS Dolphin in Gosport. Here at Gourock alongside the Admiralty pier in April 1973 dried out for bottom cleaning. This jetty was used by USN personnel travelling back and forth by boat to the Holy Loch base.

MV *Seamoor*, 1942, Wivenhoe Shipyard, built as wooden minesweeper MMS 86. 1945-1946: To Danish Navy. 1959: To Air Ministry as *Seamoor*. Sold for use as salvage vessel *Celtic Lord*, scrapped at St Davids on the Forth 1982. Lying alongside boom defence vessel *Barnard*.

AUXSY *Varangian*, 1960, James Smith, Lerwick, Shetland. Wooden cutter rigged yacht 32ft long built on traditional Shetland double ended clinker lines. 1976: Bought from Gareloch by a Shetlander Gordon Smith, and sailed to New Zealand mostly single handed.

SS *Weather Observer*, 1940, Hall Russell, Aberdeen Built as Flower Class Corvette HMS *Marguerite* K54. 1947: Ocean Weather Ship *Weather Observer*. The weather balloons were inflated in the large deckhouse aft, the Ocean Weather ships were based in James Watt Dock until 1981. 1961: Scrapped Ghent.

SS *Weather Reporter*, 1944, A.&J. Inglis, Pointhouse, as Castle Class Frigate HMS *Oakham Castle* K530. 1957: Ocean Weather Ship *Weather Reporter*. 1977: Middlesborough for scrapping.

MV *Cloch*, 1967, Ailsa of Troon, for Clyde Pilots when based at Gourock. River pilots normally boarded ships just opposite Gourock Pier. Her original Rolls-Royce engine was particularly noisy, and was later replaced by a Caterpillar diesel. Now fitted with gas tanks, and used to recharge the channel buoy lights on the Clyde.

TSMV *Grace Paterson Ritchie*, 70-002, 1965, Yarrow at Scotstoun. The RNLI built three boats able to stay at sea for days at a time designed on fishing boat lines by R.A. Oakley, Bideford Shipyard building one. This class were 71ft. long of steel and non self-righting. 1975: Visited Faroes. 1989: Sold to Nat. Lifesaving Assoc. of Iceland.

Vema, 1923, Burmeister & Wain, Copenhagen, as a three-masted schooner yacht *Hussar* for financier E.F. Hutton. 1926: Sold to ship owner Unnger Vetlesen, re-named *Vema*. Taken over and used by US Coast Guard as patrol vessel during the Second World War, and as barracks and training vessel. 1953: Chartered by Columbia University for Oceanographic work, then purchased. January 1976 logged millionth mile as research vessel.

122

Last two wooden MFV's working on the Clyde. MFV 15 was a 61.5ft boat built by Mashford Bros, Cremyll, in 1942, and the smaller 45ft boat was built by J. Bolson at Poole in 1945. It can be seen that MFV 15 has had her wheelhouse moved forward. Salvage and mooring vessel *Salmoor* and lifting pontoon behind.

Torch, 1964, Sonderborg Skibs. A/S Sonderborg. Built as *Mistralen*, then *Hathershus* in 1966, *Leise Nova* 1971, *Ceresi* 1976 and *River Avoca* in 1976 and owned by R.V.T. Hall, Dublin. Replaced the steam driven *Torch* in 1978 and took her name for buoyage duties. A special crane was fitted, and a repainted buoy and gas storage tanks can be seen on deck.

Fore deck of steam puffer, showing fore deck arrangement. In the background is Cartsburn Street, leading up to the former site of Scotts Shipbuilding & Engineering Co. Ltd's engine works. This street had its own rail line leading from the works down to the shipyard. The engine works were in front and behind the dark line of the Gourock-Glasgow railway line.

One of the fire monitors on the Clyde Shipping Company's tug MV *Flying Phantom*. The water/foam supply pipe leads up the centre, and nozzle barrel actuating control cylinders are mounted on the head. Built in 1981 by Ferguson Bros, she was fitted with a retractable bow thruster in 1997. Transferred to Cory Towage Ltd in 2000.

TSDEMV *Scotia*, 1971, Ferguson Bros, Port Glasgow, for Ministry of Agriculture & Food Dept, Leith, as a fishery research and survey vessel. Replaced by new vessel of same name in 2000 and then sold to Italy. Seen in Garvel Dry-dock Greenock, note the bulbous bow.

AUXSV *Prince Louis*, 1944, Ring Anderson, at Svendborg, as the three mast schooner cargo vessel *Nette S*, then *Annette S*. Later *Peder Most* owned by A.E. Sorensen. 1955: To Moray Sea School of Burghead and renamed *Prince Louis*. 1968: To French religious charity organisation, renamed *Belle Espoir II*. 1993-1994: Rebuilt. Shown in James Watt Dock in April 1967, with *Clan Finlay* fitting out in the background.

Ulva and RASC *Mull* seen in the Albert Harbour. *Mull* was completed as Isles Class A/S M/S trawler HMS *Mull* T110 by Cook, Welton & Gemmell at Beverley in 1941. 1946: To R.A.S.C. Ministry of Defence Army Dept, on wreck dispersal. 1962: Aground at Tarbet, salved and then sold out of service in 1974.

Typical scene in East India Harbour, with vessels laid up and repairing adjacent to James Lamont's repair works and dry-docks. *Maid of Argyll*, motorised puffer *Lady Morven*, MacBrayne's *Lochiel* with Fishery Protection vessel *Brenda* outboard. All of these warehouses and houses have now been knocked down.

Clansman (2), 1964, Hall Russell, Aberdeen, for David MacBrayne, second of three similar car ferries by this builder to serve the Western Isles. Owned by the Secretary of State, hence Leith registry. Adjustable car ramp allowed for operation at any state of tide. 1969: Was a floating exhibition ship in the Thames as centrepiece of 'Highland Fling' Exhibition. 1972-1973: Converted to drive through and lengthened by 36ft for Ullapool-Stornoway service. 1976: Operated on the Ardrossan-Brodick route. 1984: To Torbay Seaways and later operated as pilgrim ship at Gulf of Aquaba as *Al-Hussein*. In Garvel Dry-dock Greenock, before conversion.

This was all that remained of the world famous shipyards of Scotts Shipbuilding & Engineering Company after demolition in 1987. The opening on the left led to Scotts' dry-dock, with the former fitting out basin in the centre having been filled in, the sloping cleared areas to right are where once the launching ways and fabrication sheds once stood, the main Greenock-Glasgow road is at the bottom of the picture. Offices have now been built on the site, with a riverside walkway.

This spectacle is a sad reminder of site where in a period of over 200 years Scotts', Robert Steele and Greenock Dockyard built thousands of ships for the Four Corners of the world.

John Scott started a shipyard in Greenock in 1711, and was unique in that there was an unbroken line of succession of the Scott family associated with the company until take over by British Shipbuilders in 1977.

The range of ships built included pioneering steamers, clippers, West Indiamen, four masted barques, early Dreadnoughts, cruisers, destroyers, submarines, high class cargo and passenger ships, drill ships, RFA's tankers, bulk carriers and many intermediate specialist types. Engines were also constructed from earliest days until demise.

This view can perhaps sum up the retreat from major shipbuilding on the lower reaches of the Clyde, by the end of the nineteen eighties only empty sheds, where remaining, were a reminder of what was. In the sixties and early seventies the river was a hive of commercial activity. Ships continued to be built in the numerous yards along the banks of the Clyde, and a steady flow of vessels moved up and down the river with cargo to and from ports all round the world.

This in turn stimulated the ancillary activities of puffers, tugs, coasters and other specialist craft, all of which made the lower reaches of the river a paradise for the ship-lovers and photographers of all ages.

Alas, this was to be the end of the halcyon days, shipyards began to close down, and the remorseless advance of container traffic and roll-on roll-off cargo movements hastened the end of traditional cargo handling.

Hopefully the images on these pages will capture the diversity of types of ships seen in the ten years from the mid 1960s. Luckily I was on hand to record many of these with my camera, both from ashore and afloat, and with a couple of exceptions I took them all around Greenock and the Firth of Clyde.